HOW TO MAKE A
MUMMY

Contents

Badger
LEARNING

Vocabulary

afterlife

bandages

Egyptians

embalmer

linen

mummify

Pharaohs

pyramids

1. MEET THE EMBALMER

Welcome to Ancient Egypt. I'm an embalmer.
That means that I make mummies out of dead bodies.

Ancient Egyptians believe that after you die you enter a new world called the afterlife where you will need your old body to survive.

But dead bodies soon rot away so, to make them last, we turn them into mummies.

It can take up to 70 days to make a mummy.

Do you want to know how it's done?

2. MUMMY MAKER

I love my job, but sometimes it gets a bit disgusting.

I hope you don't mind touching blood and guts.

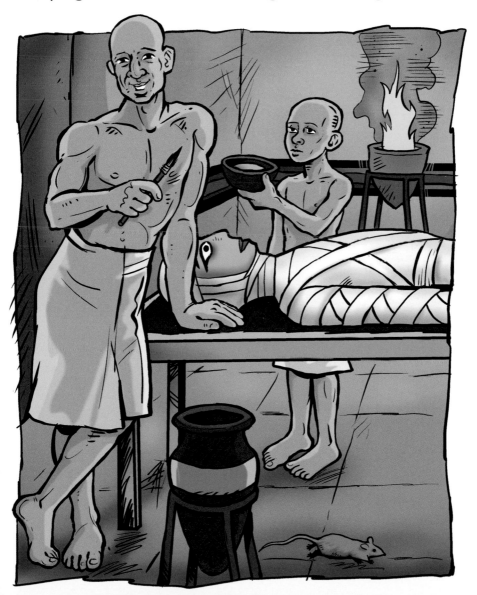

Step one

First of all you need to bring the body to my workshop. This is known as 'The Beautiful House'!

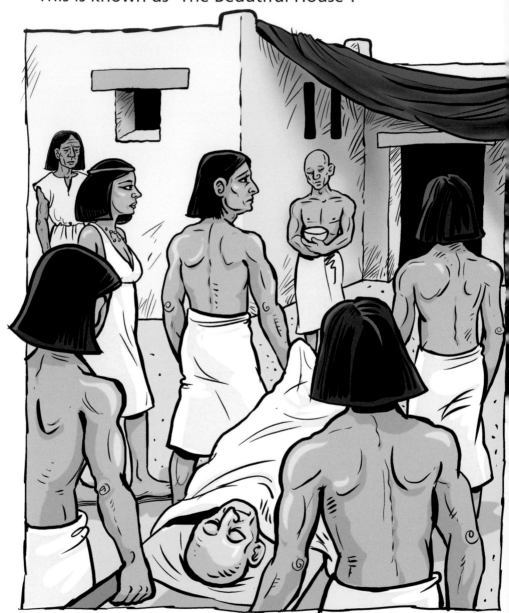

Step two

Lay the body out on a table and make a small cut in its left side.

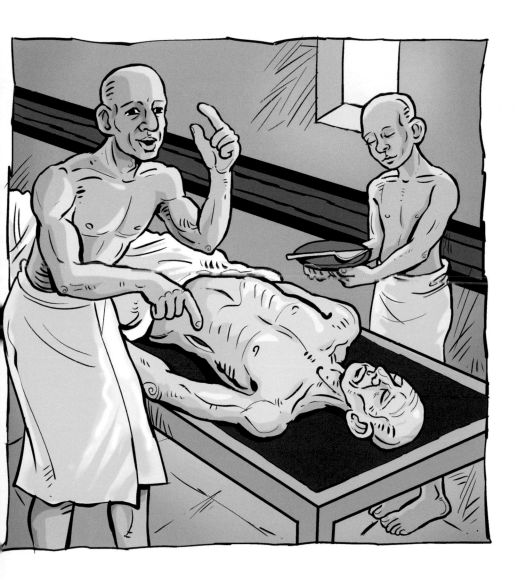

Step three

Now comes the gross bit.

You need to pull out the liver, lungs, stomach and even the long wiggly guts through the cut.

These slimy bits are stored in special jars. Each jar has the head of a different god as its lid.

The human-headed god looks after the liver.

The baboon-headed god looks after the lungs.

The jackal-headed god looks after the stomach.

The falcon-headed god looks after the guts.

Step four

Now it gets really yucky.

Take a long metal hook and stick it up the nose. You need to wiggle it about until the brain is all mashed up. Now you can pull the brain out of the nostrils!

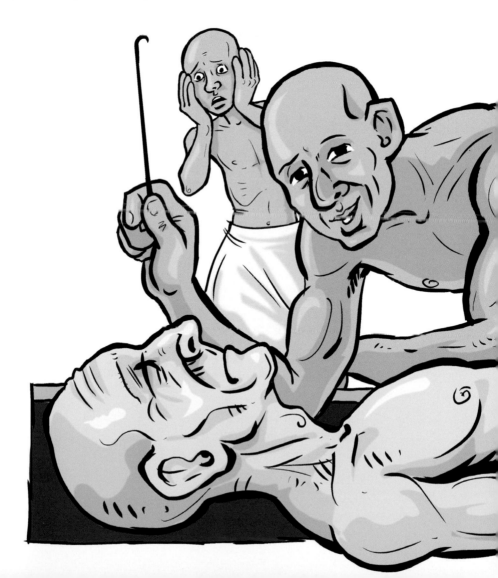

It doesn't matter that the brain is all mashed up when you pull it through the nostrils. We just throw it away.

After all, the brain is not an important part of the body, is it?

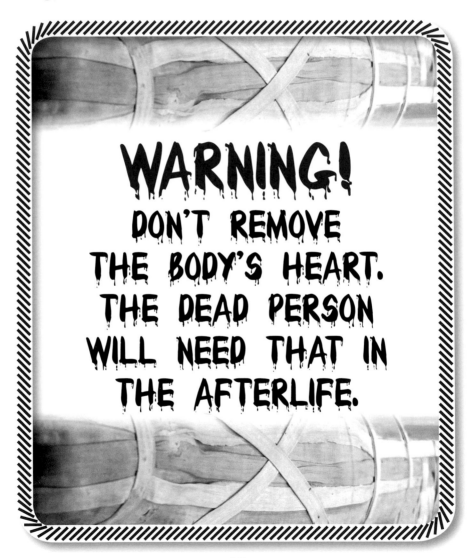

WARNING!
DON'T REMOVE
THE BODY'S HEART.
THE DEAD PERSON
WILL NEED THAT IN
THE AFTERLIFE.

Step five

The next job is to pack the body in a special salt and leave it to dry for 40 days.

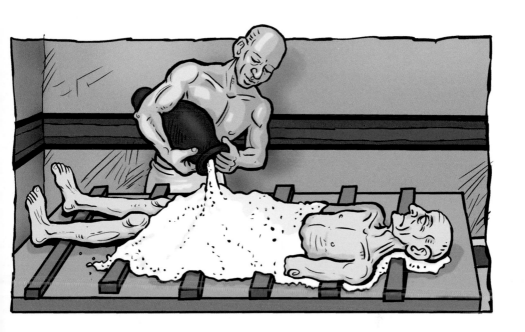

You will have to stand guard to make sure wild dogs don't try to eat it!

Step six

After 40 days, you need to wash the body using water from the River Nile.

Then you rub in special oils to keep the skin looking nice and fresh.

Step seven

You need to stuff the body with sawdust, leaves and cloth so that it looks lifelike!

Sometimes we put black stones in the place of eyeballs. One king even had his eyes replaced with raw onions!

We also use onion skin to plug the mummy's nostrils!

Step eight

Tie thread around the mummy's fingernails and toenails so they don't fall off.

Step nine

Finally, it's time to wrap the mummy in linen bandages. The bandages stop the mummy falling apart in its tomb.

It will take you about a week to wrap a mummy.

WOW! facts

It takes 372 square metres of cloth to wrap a mummy. (That's enough to cover a 25 metre swimming pool.)

Step ten

The next thing to do is to take your freshly-wrapped mummy and put it in a coffin.

Paint two eyes on the coffin. Then put the mummy in the coffin so its face is lined up with the painted eyes on the outside.

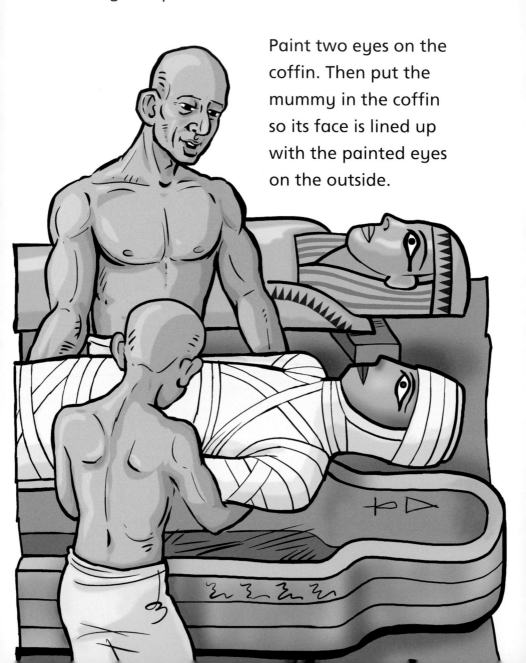

3. INTO THE TOMB

Once the mummy is made, it is taken to its tomb.

Pharaohs used to build themselves huge pyramids, but robbers stole all the treasures that were buried with them.

Now, we hide the mummies in tombs under the ground.

It's not just humans that we turn into mummies.
Some Egyptians ask us to mummify
their cats and dogs too.

We also mummify animals that people offer as gifts to the gods in the temples.

Sometimes snakes, apes, fish and even crocodiles are mummified.

In fact, we will mummify anything if the price is right!

There aren't always enough animals to go around. Some embalmers make fake mummy cats out of sticks and old rags.

The people wanting gifts for the gods can't tell what is a real mummified animal and what is a fake so they buy them anyway.

Those con artists had better watch out.

Remember I told you not to remove the mummy's heart? Ancient Egyptians believe that the gods weigh your heart on a special set of golden scales when you die.

If you have
lived a good life,
your heart will
weigh less than
a feather.

You will be let
into the afterlife.
Result!

But if you've been bad, and your heart is heavy, you won't be allowed in.

Worst of all, a scary monster will gobble up your heart.

I don't fancy that, but I'm not worried. My mother taught me to be honest and a good embalmer always listens to his mummy!

So that's all there is to it! If you don't mind the smell of dead bodies and you don't mind touching blood and guts, come and work for me as an embalmer.

Questions

How long does it take to make a mummy? *(page 8)*

What part of the human body is placed inside the jackal-headed jar? *(page 14)*

How is the brain removed? *(page 15)*

How long is the body packed in salt for? *(page 17)*

What other things were mummified? *(pages 24 and 25)*

What did the ancient Egyptians believe would happen to your heart if you had lived a bad life? *(page 29)*

INDEX